WOO HOO!

Hey Mel,
Saw this in the store + started reading. Couldn't put it down so I had to buy it. Hope you know how

A Gift For:

proud we are

Melanie

of you +
how excited we are for

From:

you as you

Aunt Jayne

start the
next chapter of your life. Always remember—
Anything is possible if you believe in yourself.   XOXO

Published by Hallmark Gift Books,
a division of Hallmark Cards, Inc.,
Kansas City, MO 64141
Visit us on the Web at Hallmark.com.

Editorial Director: Delia Berrigan
Editor: Jennifer Snuggs
Art Director: Chris Opheim
Designer: Rob Latimer
Production Designer: Bryan Ring

ISBN: 978-1-59530-582-4
GGT1332

Printed and bound in China

she's graduating!

Advice and Wisdom
From **77** Friends of Hallmark

Table of Contents

i wish i'd known then (what i know now)

One of the most important things you will learn in your lifetime is to trust yourself. You may be young, and you may think that you are inexperienced. But by the time you turn 18, you already have a good idea about who you are and what you have the potential to achieve.

Now unfortunately, I did not realize this when I graduated from high school. I went off to college and for the first time in my life, felt like I was lost at sea. College can be a pretty confusing place for anyone, and it certainly was for me. I encountered hundreds of ideas, perspectives, and ways of being, and I started to think that perhaps my own didn't measure up.

It took me a few years and many experiences to get to the point where I felt comfortable about what I believed in and what I wanted out of life. And funnily enough, I found myself exactly where I had been upon my graduation from high school.

At the age of 23, I found that I was the same person I had been at the age of 18 years. The main difference was that I had some life experiences to back up my beliefs and perspectives, so I was more confident about them.

Thinking about that makes me realize that at 18, I already had good instincts about right and wrong and about what I could achieve. And it makes me think that you do, too. You are not going out into the world empty-handed. Your perspectives matter. You matter. Things will be difficult sometimes, and you may find yourself questioning everything you have ever believed. But trust in yourself. You already have the tools to help you make the most important decisions in your life.

ROSE ATIENO – WATERLOO, IA

Don't ever be afraid of change.

I thought I should be a teacher, a nurse, or a secretary because that's what women became when I graduated. No one ever told me I had the option to switch careers as I grew and learned about the world.

I've been a counselor, a store owner, a social worker, and a real estate agent, and I am waiting for my next career.

Change can be freeing. Change can be exhilarating. Change can save your life. If you see an opportunity—go for it.

TERRI TIFFANY – ROUND ROCK, TX

Don't move out of your parents' home
until you are certain you're ready.
If there is one thing more embarrassing
than still living with your parents at thirty,
it's moving back in with them at thirty-one!

CONNIE PULLEN – EAGLE CREEK, OR

As you graduate, I want you to know that life is not a sprint; it's a marathon. I wish I had known that.

Don't be in a hurry to "get through" anything. Every stage has its own lessons to be learned. They also have their own joys to be enjoyed. Savor it all!

Don't rush it, slow down! Make the right choices no matter how long they take. Find the right person, not just the available person. Just because you have been with someone for a long time doesn't mean you are meant to stay with that person. Unless you have a passionate need to be married to that person, move on, even if it scares you. Move on and find someone who will take your breath away. Someone who will make your heart beat fast. Don't settle; move on. Wait; don't rush.

Find the right job. Don't settle for the job that pays OK but doesn't satisfy your curiosity or drains your spirit. If your job does that, move on. Find another job even if it scares you. Find a job that excites you and makes you energized to get up in the morning. A job that you love to go to every day. Don't settle; move on. Wait; don't rush.

Find the right place to live, not just the first available place. Make sure you will like coming home. Make it a safe haven. Make sure your home is something you're proud of and not just a place to put your stuff. Wait and buy good furniture, not just something that comes out of a box. Buy furniture that requires a delivery truck to deliver it. Don't settle. Wait; don't rush.

These are the things I learned but wish I had known.

COLEEN MCCREA KATZ - HAVERTOWN, PA

I wish I'd known that going to work was virtually the same as going to high school.

You still have to get up at the crack o' dawn to get there on time. The powers that be are still handing out assignments. The social dynamics are the same: there's still a popular group, the overachievers, the loners, and the geeks/nerds. And we're still not sure what the Mystery Meat that they're serving in the cafeteria is.

The only difference between the two is that you don't get summers off from work.

JOELLE BEEBE – MOUNT PLEASANT, MI

If I knew then what I know now, I would have tried harder to learn patience.

There are plenty of times I've needed math and science but not as often as I've needed patience. Traffic jams, slow waiters, crowded festivals—they all require patience. If I had known how many hours of my adult life would be spent waiting, I would have trained for it!

I really do admire people who can calmly cope when things don't go right. They're the ones who pull out a book when a flight is delayed. I stare at a bug on the wall. Patient people play flashlight tag during power failures. I alternate between flicking the light switch and pressing the remote. When patient people are put on hold, they hum and make grocery lists. I snap pencils.

I'm trying to change, but change takes time. And wouldn't you know it, it also takes patience!

RYAN FOSNOW – TEGA CAY, SC

I'm sitting here at the age of 33 watching my toddler build a tower with blocks. I wonder how this all happened, this being a grown-up thing. Don't get me wrong, I love being a wife, being a mother to an 18-month-old, and having a baby on the way. I'm currently in my third career and have an amazing life, but it seems like just yesterday I was 18 and graduating from high school. I wish I had known how fast it would go.

Don't be in a hurry. There may be times where days feel like an eternity, such as the countdown 'til you move out of your parents' house. But I promise, you will blink and be in your 30s and wonder how it all went by so fast.

Don't be in a hurry. Enjoy 18, 21, 25 . . . all those milestone birthdays. More important, enjoy the freedom you will have in your youth—going to college and being able to focus on just you.

Don't be in a hurry. Put time into your new friendships. Take a nap in the grass after math class. Stay up late talking about your future with your boyfriend, but you don't have to have a perfect plan right now. Travel to other countries. What you discover might change the way you see the world.

I was always in a hurry to grow up, to move on, for what was next to come. I was always planning and prepping for the next day, the next event, the next milestone. I missed out on a whole lot of fun. You will get there. I promise.

Be present in your daily life. Breathe. Relax. Being a grown-up will come soon enough, and you will never get this time back. Go have some adventures you can tell your future children about someday. Take your time. Laugh. Explore the incredible world around you. It's something you'll never regret.

REBECCA KYLE – DRIPPING SPRINGS, TX

Parking tickets. I was given more than my fair share when I was in college. The parking police even got new scooters while I was there, and I know I helped with funding from all of the fines I paid.

I look at money differently now, and at $50 a ticket, I realize I could have saved gobs of dollars if I would have been more responsible. No doubt that the university was pleased with my additional financial contribution, but I now wish I would have taken the extra 15 minutes to park in the right lot.

My advice to you is park where you are supposed to and begin saving money while you are in school. You'll be thankful for the extra cash in your pocket and your bank account.

DEVANEE CHAPMAN – BOERNE, TX

Always strategically place any tattoos in locations on your body that can easily be covered up later in life. Why? Because areas on your body tend to go south as you age and explaining to your grandchildren (and yes, you will probably have some) that "No, dear, that is a butterfly, not a pterodactyl," is a conversation no grandmother wants to have!

REBECCA MEINDERS – PECATONICA, IL

I worked lunches during the week in a small deli that sold made-to-order, carry-out subs. Fridays were usually busy, but one Friday we were slammed. There wasn't a spare second to stop and take a breath, let alone tidy up. The floor was littered with bits of lettuce and other food, and the customer line never seemed to shorten. The three of us behind the counter hurried to fill the many lunch-hour orders.

It was late when the rush finally tapered off. I was hungry. My legs and back ached. The area behind the counter was in chaos.

With a sigh, we started cleaning. The last duties of our day were to restock the vegetable bins with sandwich fixings and condiments and make some Italian subs for the self-service case.

When we finished the subs, we gave a collective sigh of relief as we untied our aprons. Before we could put them away, a woman walked in. She headed straight for the self-service case and bought every single one of the Italian subs I'd just wrapped. I wanted to sit on the floor and cry as she took them out the door. Instead, I tiredly put my apron back on and once again began slicing meat and cutting vegetables and once again started making subs.

I was annoyed when the phone rang a few minutes later. Please! No more orders. I want to go home! The woman's voice on the line was cheerful.

"I just bought some of your Italian subs for our meeting," she said. "I wanted you to know they're the best subs we've ever had! You all do a great job. Thank you so much!"

Her words were few, but what a difference they made! My tiredness was gone. The day was brighter. I almost wanted to break into song. (Almost.) The call took only a few seconds, but I still remember it more than 30 years later.

As you conquer the world, let me pass along what I learned that day. Never let the chance to show appreciation pass you by. Give someone a smile, a pat on the back, or a sincere thank-you. It's often the small things that make the biggest difference.

MICHELE IVY DAVIS – ESCONDIDO, CA

I graduated high school in 1982, the same year that *Time* magazine named the personal computer "Man of the Year." I remember my math teacher saying how PCs would change the world. How these efficient machines would soon do all the monotonous, trivial work while people enjoyed long, leisurely hours at the beach. He said we'd spend quality time with our families. Pursue social causes. And do all the things that really mattered in life.

Thirty years later, I am wired 24/7. I have three phone numbers, two e-mail addresses, multiple social networks, and a Twitter account I don't even know how to use. I take my laptop to the beach, because in a global marketplace the work never ends. My car talks to me while I'm driving. My e-bills are paid with money I never see. My teenagers text me from their bedrooms. And I almost lost my job the other day because I forgot to "like" the picture of my client's Asiago bagel.

So what do I wish I'd known back in 1982? Before I got my degree in information systems? That whatever technology the future holds, it probably won't slow life down. Or make things easier. Or help people focus on what really matters.

Only you can do that. And if you do, you'll change the world.

MADELEINE KUDERICK – PALM HARBOR, FL

I wish I'd known then what I know now, that life is all about embracing change, enjoying the moment, and learning from your mistakes. That there's no such thing as perfection, and all any of us can do is be our best.

I wish I knew that friends would come and go and that sometimes letting go is better than holding on.

I wish someone had told me just how broken a heart can feel, but that it's never a reason to give up on love.

I wish I knew that how I felt about myself on the inside was a direct reflection of how I felt about myself on the outside.

I wish I knew that I had the power to define myself and not be defined by anyone else.

I wish I'd known then what I know now, that the gift of being yourself, trusting yourself, and loving yourself is the greatest gift you will ever receive.

Congratulations on your amazing accomplishment!

TERRA WALLACE – STOCKBRIDGE, GA

I wish I'd known then that my dreams were always in my grasp.
I wish I'd known then that I would get the answers, if only I would ask.

I wish I'd known then that my mother was always right.
If I'd known then what I know now, it would have prevented a fight.

I wish I'd known then the importance of knowing and loving myself.
I wish I'd known then that books weren't just a decoration on a shelf.

I wish I'd known then that the reflection in the mirror isn't who I am.
I wish I'd known then that my soul was only caught in a traffic jam.

On the contrary, if I'd known then what I know now,
life lessons wouldn't have been learned, and growth
wouldn't have been allowed.

JASON CUSATI - PROVIDENCE, RI

I wish that I would have known

that life did not have a rewind button,

and that many choices

that you make when you are young

can definitely change the outcome

of your future.

ANNETTE PEREZ – WEST PALM BEACH, FL

I wish I'd known what I know now
would have read the books
not concentrated on the looks
instead of trying to be streetwise
and flirting with the guys
knowledge should have been my prize

Instead of an A in Anatomy
should have studied History
was also good at chemistry
learned quickly about biology
along came a bouncing baby
a joy and blessing but too early

Be the best you, you can be
independent, confident, and happy
rise to your potential
self-esteem essential
oh, if I only knew this then
but then this poem I couldn't pen

Susan Burns – Tallaght, Ireland

My first credit card:
the spark to my fuse.
So many things I wanted.
So much I could use.

I shopped 'til I dropped
and acted like a fool.
I thought I was winning,
but all I did was lose.

Your credit won't disappear.
It's an incredible tool.
So handle it with care
and never with abuse.

Don't put your name on the line
without reading the rules.
It's a statement you take everywhere.
Make sure it's good news!

MICHELLE TRANI – RIVERSIDE, NJ

Stay curious!
Learn something new every day.
Ask a question so that
you can continue to learn.
Learning and growing
keep you motivated
to become a better person.

CINDY STRINE – COLUMBIA, MO

I wish I had known that I did not have to grow up instantly. Take a little time to be young and be yourself. Travel and explore now while you do not have children or a spouse waiting for you at home. Be silly and have fun. You have your whole life to be responsible and serious. Don't be in such a hurry to grow up: Marriage and children will be waiting for you when you are ready. Take the time to figure out who you are before you let the roles of mother and wife define it for you.

SIERRA RENDON – COTTONWOOD, CA

I know it's hard, but fight against the urge to look to other people to define who you are and to validate whether you're OK or good enough. Sure, ask people you value for feedback and insight, but don't look to them to reflect who you are.

As you go through life's experiences, you'll begin to uncover what you truly enjoy doing, what inspires you, what makes you feel confident. Trust those instincts to solidify who you are. If you look to others to define you, you will constantly be searching for a sense of your identity and feeling ungrounded.

Accept yourself in all your strengths and weaknesses—they define who you are: a one-of-a-kind person. There's no one else like you in this world!

PATTY PARK – STEVENSON RANCH, CA

THE CLIFFNOTES VERSION
FOR EASY CRUISING ALONG THE ROAD OF LIFE:

- NEVER compromise who you are for who others want you to be.
- Paper is always better than plastic—both environmentally and financially.
- Once you hit send, there is no going back.
- Don't be obsessed with the scale. Your kind heart weighs more than you think.
- Men are like sunglasses. Do you ever buy the first pair you try on? Try on a bunch of pairs, and settle on the one that fits you best.
- Words can hurt more than a punch to the stomach. Choose your words carefully.
- Don't judge others unless you have a robe on and gavel in your hand.
- Integrity is doing what is right when no one is watching.
- Exercise is your friend. Always make time for friends.
- There is no redo on yesterday. Forget about it. However, don't make the same mistakes tomorrow.

JILL WASHBURN — JACKSON, WI

I wish I'd known then (what I know now)
that "true love" happens when you
least expect it and, more important,
when you aren't looking for it
to show up at a frat party!

PEGGY VINCENT – EAST FALLOWFIELD, PA

What I did know then is that iodine and baby oil work great together for getting a deep, dark tan. What I didn't know then is that wrinkles are not the same as character lines.

Character lines will get you much further in life, so work on your character, not your tan. And always wear sunscreen!

DARLENE M. PLUMMER — FORT WRIGHT, KY

I wish I would have known that the friends you make in high school don't always last. They matter a lot and give you great memories to look back on, but when you walk across that stage, everything changes. People go separate ways, and friendships that once were very strong, now barely exist. So, after you graduate, make sure to be open and create new friendships in this next phase of your life!

ALINA PECK – FORT MILL, SC

I wish I'd known what my true bliss was at the age of 18. Actually, I did know—I wanted to be a Broadway star! Instead, I listened to the adults in my life who said, "Not gonna happen! Too much competition. If you must major in music, teach!" In other words, "You're not good enough."

Never limit yourself! Don't listen to naysayers. Do what you want to do. Go to a school or college that will help you get there. Hang with people who share your interests. Of course, you'll wind up competing with them, but competition's healthy—it makes you work harder!

Keep your eye on your goal, girl! Marriage can wait. Having children can wait. When you're young, you have time to try! You can make mistakes—that's how you learn. But do not make the mistake of abandoning your dreams until you've given it all you've got!

Now get out there and get going!

MARY LOU BALDWIN – AMSTERDAM, NY

I wish I'd known how much
one single kind word or
simple smile could impact
another person's life.
I may have taken the time
to do that a little more often.

DEANA TAYLOR – BATH, IL

I wish I'd known as a recent graduate that the body cannot survive on sugar and pizza alone! I would've looked better, felt better, and had more energy had I known and believed this.

Learn from me, recent grads—the "parental controls" are now off, so exercising and maintaining (or creating) a healthy diet are now your responsibility. It will take time and energy to sort through the cafeteria options or cook for yourself, but with effort, you can do it, and it will be worth it because you will look and feel great!

A few more words of wisdom: frozen fruits and vegetables work just as well as fresh ones, and make sure you pack easy, nutritious snacks in your backpack. Sandwiches, apples, bananas, raw almonds, and hard-boiled eggs are quick, easy, effective ways to get nutrients in your body so you can maintain your busy schedule. Plus, think how awesome you'll look in your bathing suit on a tropical vacation or spring break!

REBECCA HILL – LOS ANGELES, CA

If I could turn back the hands of time,
Would I make changes to this life of mine?
Knowing the things that I know now,
I think my life would be different somehow.

Of course, I wouldn't trade my children or friends,
But just some of the means and some of the ends.
I'd work real hard at my jobs and all,
But I'd be more available when friends did call.

My priorities would have changed a bit.
Into the wee hours at work I wouldn't sit.
I would have said, "I love you" more
Of course, back then, who kept score!

So what exactly am I trying to say?
"Don't put off your life, not even for a day."
"There's always tomorrow," you've heard that one.
But what if tomorrow just doesn't come?

If a friend should call for help today,
Just smile and say, "I'm on my way!"
Don't think, "I want to relax in my chair."
Get off your butt and rush to be there.

If your parents call and invite you out,
Don't moan and groan or even shout.
Just be with them as much as you can.
Someday they won't call, and then . . .?

I don't like living life in a rearview mirror,
But sometimes looking back can make things clearer.
Money and time are quickly lost,
But don't lose your friends and family at any cost.

Be you, just you, don't try to be more.
People will like you without it being a chore.
Be ready to say at the end of the day,
"I did a good job, and I like it that way."

CHRIS ZASTROW – WAUKESHA, WI

When you're young, the world seems huge. If I'd only known at your age how small it really is, I could have saved myself many embarrassing moments.

Remember that telling your boss about the geek from the grocery store, the guy that drives you crazy, might end with you sticking your foot in your mouth when you find out you're talking about your boss's favorite son.

Think before you say anything about anyone. This world really is a small place. Trust me, it's no fun learning that the hard way.

JILL BURNS – WARDENSVILLE, WV

You're better off having
a sense of humor than a plan.
Things rarely go as planned,
and while laughing may not
solve all your problems,
it will at least keep you
from pulling your hair out.

KRISTEN GIBLIN – ABERDEEN, NJ

It was 8 a.m. on a Tuesday morning, and I was sitting in the very back of my first college class. I was nervous, excited, and mostly, attempting to blend into the wall. Coming from a small school, I was intimidated by the university's sprawling campus. Everyone knew that college was serious business, or so I thought. I was proven wrong for the first of several times my freshman year as my professor entered the room.

Instead of the buttoned-up, clean-shaven educator I was expecting, a short, flamboyant man in an oversized sweater sashayed into the classroom. He stepped up to a dismally unorganized desk and bestowed his first words of wisdom (flourishing his hands over his head), "Welcome! College is just one big Lust Hotel and do not worry, there are plenty of vacancies." He threw in a wink for dramatic effect.

Have fun kissing a few frogs before you worry about finding your Knight in Shining Armor. Sir Polo Shirt, Captain Beer Pong, Mr. Perpetual Sunglasses, and Lord Lazy ("Hey Babe, can I copy your homework?") may not be Prince Charming, but they can be pretty fun. You will learn a lot about yourself and have the great stories for years to come.

ANA RAPIN – SAINT LOUIS, MI

GREAT WORDS OF WISDOM:

Always wear nice, clean underwear and makeup. You never know when you might need some medical attention from that gorgeous fireman.

BARBARA HANSEN - HIGLANDS RANCH, CO

Nothing jump-starts you
on the path to success
like a fabulous pair of shoes
for the journey!

LINDSAY ROOK – TALLAHASSEE, FL

At 16, you felt like your world would crumble if you didn't get asked to prom.

At 19, all that seems to matter is passing for 21.

At 25, you're dating the wrong guy, know it, but stay with him anyway until you come to your senses and realize you're "wasting your precious 20's on him."

And at 30, you look back on it all and laugh.

Laugh at the fact that you wish you still got carded, laugh at how you "thought" you loved him, and laugh at how time seems to fly by more every year. So, make sure you always laugh (frowns can cause wrinkles), make sure to show those around you how much you appreciate them, and please eat; do not go on every fad diet out there. Enjoy food. Enjoy life. And most of all . . . love yourself.

ANGELA FRIEND – NORTH LAS VEGAS, NV

Words of Wisdom for Your First Job:

1. Don't gossip at work; it can only lead to trouble. Don't be drawn into it.
2. Don't take your bad mood to work with you. Be cheerful; no one likes a whiner.
3. Do your best. If you make a mistake, apologize and carry on.
4. Dress appropriately—no cleavage. What are the successful people wearing? Take a hint from them.
5. Take pride in you work, whatever it is. A job well done is appreciated.
6. Be on time for work and coming back from breaks. It is noticed.

LINDA KEHLER – SCARBOROUGH, ONTARIO

Relationships are like class credits—

not all will transfer

into the next stage of your life,

but the ones that do

are worth all the effort and time

you've invested into them.

ASHLEY BERCIER – BISMARCK, ND

Nothing is more important than loving yourself. There will be times when you question your self-worth and feel like you may not be good enough, smart enough, or the dreaded pretty enough, but one day you will realize that those who questioned your abilities were fools. Those who doubted your intellect were laughable, and those who mocked your appearance were insecure.

You truly are exactly who you were meant to be . . . you. Love you, accept you, take care of you, and everything else will fall into place.

KITTY CLEMENTS – MILTON, MA

Keep moms, aunts, and all the older women who love you very close. They have your best interest at heart, have wise words, and they can usually cook you up something that will make you feel better, even if you suffer from something as serious as a broken heart.

REBECCA CHAMAA – SAN DIEGO, CA

High school is now behind you.
A bit of fashion advice before
you enter your college years:
ALWAYS wear your thinking cap
with your party shoes!

DENISE KELLER – WAUKESHA, WI

Take one last look in the mirror
before you leave home—
no one ever got the job
with her bra strap showing.

LINDA AMSTUTZ – COLUMBIA, SC

As you step out
on your own,
remember one thing—
I'll stalk you
if I don't hear from you.

Love,
Mom

KATHERINE COVEY – NINILCHIK, AK

The real world, just like school, isn't always kind. So remember to always carry extra toilet paper in your purse for those times when your best friend isn't there to hand you some under the stall when you need it.

MIKKI KRAMER – AURORA, IL

I'd like to share a little bit of advice I wish I'd known upon my graduation. It's regarding the many "fish in the sea" you're sure to encounter. Simply put, if a guy tells you he's "just not good enough for you," believe him! Then run like your butt is on fire!

JUDY COTRONE RAMIREZ – NORTH PORT, FL

A beautiful face is disfigured by an ugly tongue.
- ANCIENT MOTHER'S PROVERB

Nothing disturbs me more than to hear young ladies using foul language. It doesn't make you cool. It doesn't make you sound intelligent. It certainly isn't appropriate in the workplace. A classy woman can express herself without resorting to "cursing like a sailor."

You're probably thinking, "But everybody curses. It's no big deal anymore. Whatever!" Or maybe you're thinking in more "colorful" terms. Well, just because "everybody" does it, doesn't make it right. Strive to rise above the common and set yourself apart. Let your language be as pretty as you are.

DONNA ANDERSON – FRISCO, TX

Thelma, a kind and older woman I used to work with, knew a thing or two about how to reach your goals and see your dreams come true. She wanted the best for me so she shared this piece of her priceless wisdom with me one day.

She said, "You are young; you don't need a man and babies getting in the way of your life and career right now. Birth control and safe sex are overpriced and overrated nowadays. Let me tell you . . . all you need is an aspirin."

I looked at her with surprise and asked, "Thelma, how can an aspirin help with that?"

She replied, "Honey, you just put that tiny little pill right between your knees and hold it there!"

Trust me, it works.

SHANI FASSBENDER – COOPERSBURG, PA

An *extraordinary woman dreams* of the life she wants, then *works hard* to live it.

PAIGE LANGLEY – KINGWOOD, TX

Never marry a man
who feels threatened by your brains.
You'll have to play dumb
the rest of your life,
and there'll never be time
for anything else.

LISA LESHAW – CORAM, NY

Words to live by:

- Put your heart into the things you love.
- Put your mind into finding solutions.
- Put your soul into finding yourself.
- Put your hands out to help others.
- Put the credit card applications through a shredder.

DEANA TAYLOR – BATH, IL

the best advice i ever got

The best advice I ever got was from my father. He told me a long time ago that when you meet a new boy, make sure you get to know his family, and be especially aware of his relationship with his parents.

He said that a boy will treat you the same way he treats his mother, and he will most likely become the same type of father that his own father was.

Twenty-five years ago, I half-heartedly listened to this advice, but back then I didn't think it was fair to judge people based on who raised them. After all, you can't choose your family, right? So, I ignored this wisdom, for the most part.

Biggest mistake ever! Young ladies, choose a potential boyfriend/husband very wisely. See where he comes from, who he has associated with, who his teachers in life have been, and know his value system.

Most of us are products of our environment, and knowing someone's past is a HUGE indicator of what you can expect in your future with that person. Be smart! You're worth it!

KAREN STARKS – BARRINGTON, RI

My father's favorite line when something didn't turn out the way I had hoped was a funny variation on a famous quote. It had a deeper wisdom that took me years to appreciate:

If at first you don't succeed,
keep sucking
until you do succeed!

BOB HIVELY – CIRCLEVILLE, OH

I was always a dreamer and wanted to change the world for the better. Everyone knew this and encouraged me, but I still never did anything.

After graduation, I met a woman who was starting her own nonprofit organization. I was impressed and told her my own ambitions. She asked me what I was doing to see my dreams fulfilled. I was speechless and embarrassed because no one had ever asked me that before. She told me her grandmother always said, "Don't tell me what you are going to do. Show me what you have done." That was the most important lesson of my life.

Since then, whenever I initiate a new project, I dig in and start before I begin letting people know. By doing this, I am not only showing others I am serious, but it also says to me and the universe I am dedicated. I am proud of my successes and seeing my dreams come true.

HARVEY KIVEL — TUCSON, AZ

Upon entering the real world,
there are just three things you need to know,
according to my mother:

1. Your stuff stinks just as much as anybody else's.
2. When you point one finger at someone, you have three pointing back at you!
3. It's not what you say, it's how you say it.

DIANE HICKEY-HOTALING – VIRGINIA BEACH, VA

Sometimes
it will be necessary
to forget **how you feel**
and remember what
you are worth.

TERRI MCMILLAN – LAURINBURG, NC

Never
> write anything down that you
> don't want people to read,

never
> say something you
> don't want people to hear,

and never, ever
> take pictures of something you
> don't want people to see.

WANDA TINCKER – NORTH ATTLEBOROUGH, MA

A female gym teacher once told our class when dressing it was alright to show enough to prove you are a woman, as long as you cover enough to prove you are a lady. She also said it is alright to strive to be attractive, but not to the point of being an attraction. She was so right!

JACQUIE BUSER – CHICKASHA, OK

We've all heard the old adage "Do what you love and you'll never work a day in your life." The best advice I ever received was that's a myth!

Don't do what you love for a career; do what you're good at! I love to play golf, but I don't have the natural talents nor will I likely be able to develop the skills it takes to be a professional golfer. If I tried to become one, not only would I not succeed, I'd likely end up frustrated and lose my love for the game.

You should seek to earn your living in an area where you excel. If you're good at what you do, you'll likely rise to the top of your field, have a sense of satisfaction, and make a good living from your career. Then, you can pursue what you love as a hobby and remain passionate in your enjoyment of it.

CAMI HEPLER – HICKORY, NC

It was the last day of gym class and our teacher gathered us around her and asked that we do something for her once we graduated. We couldn't imagine what that request might be, but a lot of the girls thought she would tell us to make exercise a part of our daily lives. No, instead she gave us this advice: Every day, pick up the daily newspaper and read something from every section. If you do this, you will be considered well-rounded, and people will find you to be interesting and intelligent.

I never forgot her words, and it has been almost forty years since then. So, I started the habit of reading the newspaper, reading even sections at the time that bored me to tears. These were the business and sports sections. Now, I've come to love every part of the newspaper, and I do believe that I can talk to anyone about anything because I definitely became well-rounded by heeding her advice.

DONNA LUNNY – HAVERTOWN, PA

I recall talking to Dr. Weeston one afternoon about how I had felt the need to change my major. I then continued to tell him that I was going to take general education for a semester so I could figure out what I wanted to major in.

Dr. Weeston then responded with a smirk, "Well, when you get your whole life figured out in one semester, you give me a call and tell me how you did it." I then laughed and realized those words he said were words of wisdom.

You have your entire life to figure out who you are. Do not try to push yourself into doing something or being someone that you are not. Things will eventually fall into place.

ANDREA HAMM – SPRINGFIELD, MO

Bubbly, skinny, sweet Gail. I will never forget her. She arrived to volunteer in a long, flowing skirt with a burst of color and a heart of kindness. The kids loved her and so did I. As she arrived each week, I learned more and more about the long list of volunteer activities with which she was involved. Wow. How can you do so much, Gail?

Humbly, she explained that you have to make your life matter. "You have to validate your life," she told me.

I learned the definition of success that day. Faced with many struggles and strife in her life, this woman was carving a path through the difficulties to make a difference. Turning it around. Helping others. Making her life matter. Her wisdom has stayed with me for over twenty years.

On difficult days, I think back to those words and her vision. Although most of us will never know greatness, we can have great moments. In doing so, we know we have made something of this life. Gail's words remind me that every little bit of what I do counts. I believe it is the best advice I've ever been given.

Your life is precious . . . and so is what you bring to it. Be successful. Go, and validate your life.

NANCY DYER – WALTHAM, MA

When my stepdad drove me to college for my final drop-off at the dorms, we stopped at the drive–through of a fast food restaurant on the way. That's where I heard four words that I called upon for support over and over again during my ensuing years of education:

"Never, never, never quit."

The conversation was a bit lengthier. It went something like, "It's easy to give up, but no matter how difficult school may get, just never, never, never quit."

The advice didn't seem profound at the time, in fact, it sounded more like a warning to me then. It wasn't until I struggled with classes and feelings of aloneness that I was in the mindset to call upon the advice. The simple words of wisdom reminded me that times get tough for everyone, but none of us would achieve anything of value if we took the easy way out instead of working hard and persevering.

If times get tough for you, reach out to someone who's been through it before, and never, never, never quit.

CHRISTINE SCHULTZ – KENOSHA, WI

All through my childhood, I made up knock-knock jokes for every occasion. On the day I was graduating from high school, my mother wrote a special knock-knock joke just for me:

Knock, knock!
Who's there?
Opera.
Opera who?
Opera-tunity, and don't ever think
opportunity only knocks once.

Don't let life's detours stand in your way. Continue to pursue your dreams and success will follow.

GEORGIA HUBLEY – HENDERSON, NV

I can remember that day in class like it was yesterday. There we were, desks formed into a circle in the middle of the room, notebooks in front of us, and all attention directed to our teacher, Mr. Carle. We were getting ready to recite our writing assignment in front of the entire class. This meant that everyone would concentrate on the words and format of their story and contribute some constructive criticism to help make each paper a better piece.

Being the shy person that I am, when my turn rounded the corner I was hesitant, and then, I heard my teacher speak these words that I will never forget as long as I live: "Don't let the fear of striking out keep you from playing the game."

This one little quote has helped me to get through many tough times in my life, and today, I still would have to say it is the best advice I ever got from a teacher.

JOLENE JENNINGS – UNITY, NH

*Of course wearing mascara,
cover-up, and lipstick is nice.
Yet, a woman who wears confidence
every day will always look glamorous—
no matter the occasion.*

RUBY PINKHAM – SPARKS, NV

My grandmother always said,

    "When they say you can't, you show them you can!"

My grandmother always said,

    "You can only be a fool if you let a fool make you one!"

My grandmother always said,

    "Be rich in givin' and poor in takin'!"

My grandmother always said,

    "Now that you've become a young woman,

       don't be so fast to become someone's old lady!"

MARIE BENNETT – COATESVILLE, PA

When confronted with a problem—face it head-on. The easy thing to do is avoid a confrontation or run away from the issue. The smart thing to do is deal with it, resolve it, and move forward with your life.

Once you choose the run-away option, it makes it easier to run the next time and so goes your life—constantly running away from something.

PEGGY GARRETT – INDEPENDENCE, MO

After committing to too many clubs and events in high school, my history teacher told me that in college it was important to remember that it's "never too late to quit."

It sounded cynical at the time, but I've come to realize that there's a virtue to knowing when to say no. Say yes—be involved—but don't do so at the cost of your sanity or your happiness. You've already come this far!

KATIE MULLINS – EVANSVILLE, IN

The best advice I ever got was "Clean up as you go along."

Grandma was teaching me how to bake cookies. After measuring out some sugar, I had placed the sugar bag on the counter. She handed it to me and pointed to the cabinet.

"Clean up as you go along. That way, you won't have to deal with messes later."

I took her advice to heart not just in the kitchen but also in my relationships with others. If I "mess up" a friendship by saying or doing something hurtful, I do my best to "clean things up" right away. A heartfelt apology can wipe away a smudge before it sets into a stain.

KELLY FOSNOW – TEGA CAY, SC

The best advice I ever received came from my Great-Uncle Norman. At the time, he was in his 90s and stuck in a nursing home for almost 7 years because of failing health.

He told me, "Spend your money and have fun. I had all the money in the world and now it does me no good because I can't do anything with it."

Taking his advice to heart since graduation, I've had adventures in Europe, Mexico, Hawaii, the Caribbean, the Bahamas, and Vegas. I've opted for the best seats at many, many rock concerts (especially the Rolling Stones). I couldn't say no to skydiving and hot air ballooning, and I've even danced with a dolphin! Oh, the fun I've had!

My savings bank will never be full, but my memory bank is! Thanks, Uncle Norman!

PAULA MORTIMER – CHILTON, WI

When I was first learning how to drive, I struggled with lane placement. Depth perception had never been my strong suit, so I just guessed at where I thought the vehicle should be in the lane and stayed there—most times ending either half onto the shoulder or thrumming along the rumble strips on the center line. My mother had long since given up on teaching me, preferring to sit in the backseat and look out the rear window, leaving my father to teach me the fundamentals.

After repeated close calls, I was ready to give up. I pulled into the closest parking lot, turned off the car, and handed the keys to my dad. "I just can't do it," I reasoned. Walking never hurt anyone and surely someone would take me anywhere I really needed to go.

Ever the patient man, my dad returned the keys to me with a gentle smile and said everything would be OK and that I should picture myself where I want to be. He explained that if I could imagine myself being in the right place in the lane, then my mind would move my physical body to where I wanted/needed to be. And dang it, he was right!

That simple advice came in handy in many more occasions in my life. Do I go back for more school or get a job? If I make this decision now, how will it affect where I want to be ten years down the road? Do I buy those awesome shoes or put that money in a savings account for the future?

As you celebrate the great accomplishment of your graduation, remember to picture yourself where you want to be. And with hard work and a little luck, you'll end up where you need to be on the road of life. Congratulations!

JOELLE BEEBE – MOUNT PLEASANT, MI

"We're not getting the house," I told my mother and grandfather as we sat in the backyard on a summer afternoon. "We signed the papers, but the owner died before he could sign them, too. It's off the market."

That house had been just what my husband and I had wanted, and it was in our price range. It was tiny and needed lots of work, but it had acreage.

My Grandpa Macdonald leaned forward in his chair and looked at me closely. "You know," he said in his softly musical Scottish brogue, "sometimes you don't get what you want on the first try. Sometimes you don't get it on the second or even the third. But don't worry. Just wait. Something better will come along." He smiled at me with confidence.

"You just don't understand," I thought. "We'll NEVER find another house." Real estate agents had already told us a house we could afford on a few acres didn't exist in our county near busy Washington, D.C.

I was so disappointed I could almost taste it.

However, Grandpa's advice stuck in my mind, and even though I had my doubts, I kept repeating his words. Something better will come along.

Then one day as I flipped through the newspaper, my finger landed on a small classified ad. And there it was. The something better!

The house listed in the paper still needed work, but it was set back on a hill, not on a busy street like the other one had been, had a great view, and its two acres were surrounded by houses and playmates for my children. We bought it the same day. Grandpa had been right.

Since that time, whenever life doesn't work out quite the way I planned or disappointment hunts me down, I remember Grandpa Macdonald's words and look forward with excitement to discover what the "something better" will be. It always appears. Grandpa packed a lot of wisdom into his five-foot frame.

In life you'll be disappointed. You'll be angry. You won't always get the job/guy/apartment you want. But don't worry. Just wait. Something better will come along. You can count on it!

MICHELE IVY DAVIS – ESCONDIDO, CA

"Look out for the curb! Look out for the tree!" Dad screamed, as I mistook the gas pedal for the brake at the shopping mall stop sign, slamming the car over the curb, and nearly wiping out a palm tree as I cut a corner too close.

The car was fine, as were Dad and I, but it was then that he told me a beautiful pearl of wisdom: "Don't ever cut corners. If you do, you'll cause a wreck."

There have been many situations in my life and career when the quickest possible option for completing a mundane task would have allowed me more time to move onto other things that were more exciting or enjoyable. However, instead of choosing those more pleasant options, I have always remembered that day behind the wheel and the tree that was nearly sacrificed because I cut a corner.

Cutting corners in every facet of life may seem like a valid short-term solution, but in the long run, doing so could wreck your career. If you opt for slow, wide turns and sound choices instead, your road to success will be smooth and damage-free!

JILL EISNAUGLE – TEXAS CITY, TX

My mom has always encouraged me to go after my dreams and to never let challenges keep me from accomplishing my goals. When I was just a young woman, she gave me the best advice that I've ever received. She told me, "Never be afraid to ask for what you want. The worst thing that could happen is that they'll tell you no!"

That day, she not only gave me courage to step out of my comfort zone, but she also taught me to never fear the word "no" again.

The first time I put this advice to the test was just after graduation. A new opening became available at my workplace, and I saw my chance for advancement. I was the youngest employee in the office and was unsure if I had the qualifications they were looking for. My mom's words of wisdom echoed in my head, so I interviewed for the promotion anyway. I got the job and soon became the youngest woman in the company to be placed into a management position.

I want you to remember that the word "no" is a tiny word that consists of just two letters. If you let the fear of rejection control you, it can prevent you from enjoying the awesomeness of a "yes" and from experiencing some incredible, life-changing opportunities. Besides, "no" doesn't necessarily mean "not ever." Sometimes it just means, "not right now."

KIMBERLY MURRAY – LIVONIA, MI

As I sat next to my dad, my knees trembling, he handed me the keys.

"You've got to learn," he said.

Sure, I had taken drivers education in school, but I wasn't given this task. This was harder, much harder. All the cars I had driven before were simple. This was different—four on the floor, '65 Mustang, his pride and joy.

"Girls don't need to drive these," I said to him.

"You'll be surprised what you need to know," was his response.

The goal for that day was to teach me to drive a stick shift. Step-by-step, he explained to me what I was to do.

"Now start the car and back out of the driveway."

My left foot on the clutch and my right leg trembling, I shifted into reverse, stepped on the gas and proceeded to stall, not once, twice, but maybe four or five times before I rolled out into the road.

My dad just smiled and held his comments to himself, never saying a word only gesturing with his hand to keep going.

"Forward," now only four times more difficult. That car certainly owned up to its name, bucking in each gear like an untamed horse.

What seemed like the entire day of endless stopping and starting was only a couple of hours. Dad knew I felt unsure of the way I handled his car.

He would look at me and smile and say, "You'll learn, don't give up."

I didn't give up, and on many occasions, I borrowed his pride and joy and drove it like I was meant to. I not only learned a new skill that day, I learned many more things that I used every day, like . . .

You don't have to be a boy to know boy stuff.

Those little things that you think you may never use, you just might need them.

Don't limit yourself in the knowledge you possess; learn and keep on learning each and every day.

Those little starts and stops are life's lessons to learn from and grow.

Hold your tongue when necessary and use your words responsibly.

Set small goals for yourself and be proud of what you have accomplished.

Above all—anything is possible.

DONNA WONDOLOSKI – OLD BRIDGE, NJ

Years ago, both of my grandmothers, my mother, my aunt, and a gem of a family friend gathered together and formed a special little organization called the Lucky Ladybugs. This group had no constitution, no bylaws, no officers, no dues, no meetings, and no national conventions. They did, however, have a motto. Just two simple words: keep breathing.

The message has been passed down to each family member and has filtered outward to close friends. It is sound advice that can be applied to ANY difficult situation, and if followed, can pretty much help you get through anything. There are many times when life will get hard or scary and all hope may seem to be lost, but if you keep these words in mind and remind yourself to keep breathing . . . you WILL make it through!

We start our lives breathing, and it is the one constant that must remain in order for us to continue on through life. Something as automatic as breathing might not seem like advice, but I've found "keep breathing" to be wise words that I repeat to myself and others on a fairly regular basis. Sometimes when life gets rough, we all just need a little reminder to breathe!

KATE STOVER – VALENCIA, PA

Set your *goals high,* and always make sure your underarms are shaved before you *reach for them.*

LISA CRISAFI – TRINITY, NC

In my formative years, my papaw used to coach me about my "little red wagon." Oftentimes when I would come to him with a trivial concern, he would say, "That's your little red wagon."

I hated that wagon, but over the years, it has served me well in regards to fears and expectations. Over time, I learned that I choose what goes in the wagon and, subsequently, how heavy it is to pull.

Usually fears go into two categories. There is fear of losing something I have or fear of not getting something I want. These fears have to be put in perspective, as they are the rocks that make the wagon hard to pull. I have to identify my fears and discover the root or the rock goes in the wagon.

Expectations are another offender that burden the wagon. I have a part in every resentment I have, even if my part is simply having an expectation of how I want another to behave or an expectation in regards to the outcome of a situation. Expectations are the precursor to resentments.

Resentments are especially heavy in the wagon. In learning to keep the rocks out of my wagon, I have discovered that it is a blast to get in the wagon and ride, and without rocks, there is even room for friends.

At Papaw's funeral, a little red wagon filled with flowers appeared. Flowers and friends are what truly belong in the wagon, and I am glad my wagon is red!

THERESA DRINNON – MARYVILLE, TN

When I was eighteen years old and had just graduated from high school, my aunt Laurel handed me a piece of paper with these words written on it by her, "The Sea is so Broad and my Vessel is so Meager."

That was one thing I loved about my dear aunt Laurel—she loved for me to figure out a good challenge. But what I didn't realize at the time was that this would be her very last gift to me, and this would be the most powerful and meaningful message that I would ever receive in my lifetime. It was meant as a life lesson to prepare me for what was ahead on my own journey.

My aunt Laurel died shortly after giving me the note, leaving me all alone to figure it out. I felt abandoned in this big world without her, like I was stranded on an island or treading water and not being able to move forward.

After some time reflecting back on the note, it finally all made sense to me. Her very last gift to me was that it didn't matter what type of vessel or boat that I traveled in, but where I sailed it to and how many waves I would conquer along the way. Even though the sea is so broad, the tiniest vessel can handle it! And whenever I find myself stranded on a desolate island, I know there is always a way off.

As the years passed, I have always remembered that note, especially when the sea gets rough. I have triumphantly conquered my share of waves throughout life, but I know that wherever my meager vessel sails me to, Aunt Laurel is right there by my side as my first mate, and we can conquer even the highest and boldest waves that come.

RITA VETSCH – MONTICELLO, MN

The paper was due on Monday. The assignment was to write our interpretation of the history of India. History was not my best subject, and I was laboring over just how to present my ideas.

With open books spread out on the kitchen table and pictures of India through the ages for inspiration, I began. When it was finished, I had a three-page poem, beautifully written, perfectly spaced. Words rhymed and were in proper order. I was ready and proud to hand in my paper.

A few days later, the history teacher handed our graded papers back to us. Excitedly, I looked at the top of the page. My face dropped. There in the space where I just knew I was going to find an "A," blazed a huge "F." How could this be? "My poem was so good," I thought. I didn't change history with creative license. I had to find out what happened.

I summoned the courage to ask the teacher why he gave my paper such a grade. He said that he knew that I was not capable of doing this kind of work and that I must have had someone else do it for me. I couldn't believe what I was hearing.

The following week things changed. He told me that he showed my poem to my English teacher. She recognized my work and told him that of course I wrote the poem. High school was not easy for me. My English teacher knew that I was struggling in some classes. She also knew that words were my way out. She may have gotten my grade changed, but her faith in me transformed my life.

Being a woman, whether furthering your education or career, isn't always easy. Stick to your convictions. If you see an injustice, ask why. Be proud of your accomplishments. When they are truly yours, no one can take them away.

CINDY PONKO – RICHFIELD, WI

While in college, I learned a valuable lesson from an unlikely source: a cat. My sister left town leaving her scroungy creature with me. This she-devil with an attitude entertained herself by hissing, scratching, and swinging on my landlord's drapes! From the get-go, she and I had decided to keep our distance. Thanks, Sis, for the cat from hell.

The day I went to meet my girlfriend, Molly, at the park, turned out to be a nightmare. When she didn't show or return my calls, I began to worry. I finally called 911 and was connected to a police station. Could I come down to the precinct? Why? Why couldn't they tell me what they had to say on the phone?

At the precinct, they told me Molly had been struck by a car and was gone. Since her parents lived across the country, would I go to the morgue and identify her? I did. It was her. I notified her parents. The whole nine yards.

Guys don't cry, right? I returned to my room in anguish. The pain was unbearable. I clutched at my stomach in agony. But the moans, like the tears flooding my face, were silent! I couldn't utter a sound!

To my disbelief, the cat slid toward me and with long, low whimpers, brushed her body back and forth against mine. Then she gently curled into my lap. Soon her wail became a song of comfort for me. She sensed my grief and shared it. Throughout the night, she never left my side.

I learned then that I should never trust first impressions. I learned again when I had rented a pad with a guy I thought was cool. He knew the foxy girls and the right pubs. He also skipped out on the rent and took my stereo.

The girl next door, whom I had considered a snob, was the one who sat with me in the hospital when I broke my ribs. She brought me lunch, my books, and my mail. The least likely to be my friend turned out to be my buddy. Who knew?

First impressions are often misleading. They are like lies ready to lure you in. Take your time getting to know someone before you jump to conclusions. Trust me. Been there!

LARRY CARTER – DALLAS, TX

Two days after college commencement, I unraveled my diploma to ready it for its frame and found a smaller piece of paper rolled up inside. My dad had created another diploma for me from "Life Lessons University" where he had me graduate top of my class. Unlike my official diploma, this one (made with love) contained stick-on pink hearts, a giant "I LOVE YOU," and in perfect penmanship, the best advice I ever received: "Learn something from every single person you meet no matter their background, education, or job. Everyone has their own little tidbits of knowledge to impart. Pay attention. You will be that much wiser."

I've never stopped listening, and you know what? I'm feeling pretty smart lately. I hope my dad is proud.

LISA LESHAW – CORAM, NY

There will be a lot of people who walk in and out of your life, and some you will call a friend for a short while, and others you will call a friend for a lifetime. As long as you hold your head up high through each of those relationships and you can say that you got a lesson or a memory that you can reflect on, or had a laugh, then each one was a success.

LISA PENNIE SIMS – CASTRO VALLEY, CA

Master the art
of convincing others
that it was
THEIR idea;
there will be times
when being right
is not as important
as getting it done.

DEANA TAYLOR – BATH, IL

The best advice I ever got is actually something you hear in school all the time, but it wasn't until my sister said it that it really resonated. Oddly enough, she didn't even say it to me as a piece of advice but rather just blurted it out while venting.

She was frustrated about a project at work that kept undergoing numerous tweaks and changes and she exclaimed, "Look, at a certain point, it's 'pencils down, people.'"

I laughed but also stopped and realized that nothing you do—whether in work or life—will ever be "finished." There will always be something more you can do on it, but chasing after perfection will only make you crazy and keep you from moving on to something else.

So just like your teachers used to tell you "pencils down" and ask you for your test, you have to tell yourself "pencils down" and trust that you've done the best you can at this, so that you can move on to whatever comes next.

KRISTEN GIBLIN — ABERDEEN, NJ

*If you have enjoyed this book
or it has touched your life in some way,
we would love to hear from you.*

Please send your comments to:
Hallmark Book Feedback
P.O. Box 419034
Mail Drop 215
Kansas City, MO 64141

Or e-mail us at:
booknotes@hallmark.com